F-FREEZING ABC

Posy Simmonds

Alfred A. Knopf   New York

For Raphael

THIS IS A BORZOI BOOK PUBLISHED BY ALFRED A. KNOPF, INC.

Copyright © 1995 by Posy Simmonds

Published in the United States by Alfred A. Knopf, Inc., New York,
and simultaneously in Canada by Random House of Canada Limited, Toronto.
Distributed by Random House, Inc., New York.
Published in Great Britain by Jonathan Cape Ltd. in 1995.

First American edition, 1996

Printed in Mexico.

Library of Congress Cataloging-in-Publication Data
Simmonds, Posy.
F-freezing ABC / Posy Simmonds. — 1st American ed.
p. cm.
Summary: An anteater, a bear, a cat, and a duck all search for a warm place to stay.
[1. Animals—Fiction. 2. Alphabet.] I. Title.
PZ7.S5913Ff   1995
[E]—dc20   95-18921

ISBN 0-679-87915-3

10 9 8 7 6 5 4 3 2 1

A-Anteater

"A-A-Atishoo!" sneezed the Anteater.
"I-it's a-absolutely ar-ar-arctic!"

B-Bear

C-Cat

"Brrr!" shivered the Bear.
"It's b-b-bitter!"
"C-cold!" complained the Cat.

D-Duck

"Shut up!" said the Duck.
"Stop moaning! There's a n-nice
w-warm house n-next door…
L-let's g-go over there."

So they all went to see the
E-Elephant.

"But of course! Come in!"
cried the Elephant.
"Make yourselves at home!"

"Stop squashing me!" wailed the Cat.
"Oh, let's go somewhere else!"

Across the fields, they found the

F-Fox.

"We're f-f-freezing!" said the Duck.
"*You* can sit by my fire," said the Fox,
licking his chops.
"N-n-no w-way!" flapped the Duck.

They called out to the
G-Goat.

"You're most welcome,"
said the Goat. "I've got a *huge*
H-House."

But the house was as cold as an ice box
and echoed with ghostly moans...

"Hmm…that was a short visit,"
grunted the Goat.

"Oooh, it's icy!" shivered the Anteater.
"L-let's go inside th-this

I-Igloo."

But there were insects hibernating in the igloo...

The Anteater jigged down to the **J-Jetty** ...and jumped!

"He can't swim, can he?" observed the **K-Kangaroo.**

"No, dumbo, he *can't!*" shrieked the Cat.

Luckily, the **L-Lion** had a life buoy.

"Getting dark!" quacked the Duck.
"Why not shelter in the lighthouse,"
suggested the Lion.

Up came the M -Moon, on came the N -Night.

The waves boomed and crashed.
The Duck panicked.
"Let's get out of here!"

"H-help!" cried the Duck. "We'll freeze to death!"

"Oooo dear!" hooted the O-Owl.

"No problem," said the P-Pig. "We know the perfect place for you."

"It's just over the hill," called the Q-Quail.

"Here you are," said the R-Rabbit.

"You'll be as snug as bugs in there!"

"Get outta my house!" screeched the

S-Skunk...

...who was trying to watch

T-Television.

Outside, a blizzard had
begun to blow.

"Here…use this U-Umbrella," said the Skunk.

"Let's g-go home!"
shivered the Cat.
"L-let's b-b-borrow this
V-Van."

But they woke up the

W-Wolf...

...who chased them through the woods.

"Help!" panted the Bear.
"Stop the Wolf…he's
after us!"

"Just you sit and listen to our

X-Xylophone!" bellowed the Y-Yak.

The Wolf nipped past the Yak and

Z-Zig-Zagged down the hill.

But he was too late.

"There you are!" cried the Elephant. "I've made your house nice and warm!"

"It's like an oven in here!" gasped the Bear. "It's roasting!" mewed the Cat. "I'm going…to…pass…out," moaned the Duck.

"Ahh! That's more like it!"